Lost Vil
of
Derbyshire

by Peter J. Naylor

ISBN 1 874754 64 0

1999

*Produced by a
member of*
THE GUILD OF
MASTER CRAFTSMEN

The Derbyshire Heritage Series

Happy Walking International Ltd.,
Unit 1, Molyneux Business Park,
Whitworth Road, Darley Dale,
Matlock, Derbyshire.
England.
DE4 2HJ

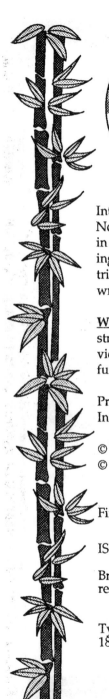

Happy Walking International Ltd.,
Unit 1,
Molyneux Business Park,
Whitworth Road,
Darley Dale,
Matlock,
Derbyshire
DE4 2HJ
Tel/Fax 01629 - 735911

Printed, bound, marketed and distributed by Happy Walking International Ltd.

© Text - Peter J. Naylor 1997.
© Photographs - as individually stated - 1997.

First Published - July 1997.

ISBN 1 874754 64 0

British Library Cataloguing-in-Publication Data. A catalogue record of this book is available from the British Library.

Typset in Avant Garde - bold, italic, and plain 10pt, 14pt and 18pt.

CONTENTS

Page No.

Acknowledgements...4

Chapter One - Introduction... 5

Chapter Two - Mythical Accounts 8

Chapter Three - Villages of Prehistory....................................11

Chapter Four - Roman Settlements 14

Chapter Five - Genocide 18

Chapter Six - Climatic Changes 22

Chapter Seven - Pestilence 25

Chapter Eight - Monastic Clearances 28

Chapter Nine - Sheep Clearances 32

Chapter Ten - The NIMBY Syndrome 35

Chapter Eleven - Inundation 41

Chapter Twelve - Urban Sprawl 45

Bibliography..48

Index..49

Other Books by Peter J. Naylor 53

The Derbyshire Heritage Series 54

Other books from Happy Walking International Ltd.,....................56

ACKNOWLEDGEMENTS

The writer wishes to record his gratitude to the following for their help in compiling this book -

Kate Froggatt for help with identifying some of the sites and walking the ground over a few of them, Phyll Jobling for correcting the manuscript and Sue Watson who collected some of the early material for me.

The Longford Church of England Primary School and the Head Teacher, Mrs. Jo Greer MA for allowing me access to the project they did on the lost villages of Hungry Bentley and Alkmonton as part of an illustrated local history trail for which they won the Wolfson Foundation Young Historian Award. A superb example of a school involving itself in its local culture.

Mr. D R Wilson, Curator, Aerial Photography Department, University of Cambridge Collection for the aerial photographs of Little Chester, Hungry Bentley, Barton Blount and Osleston. Referred to as CUC in the text.

Mr. M Murphy of Severn Trent Water, North Derbyshire District for the photograph of Ashopton and permission to use the plan of Birchinlee and the rules for the occupants.

The verses at the beginning of Chapters 1, 3, 4 and 8 are taken from Puck's Song (Puck of Pook's Hill) by Rudyard Kipling with permission.

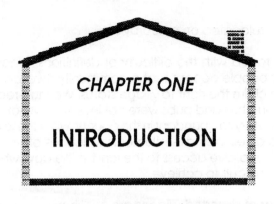

CHAPTER ONE

INTRODUCTION

"See you our pastures wide and lone,
Where the red oxen browse?
O there was a City thronged and known,
Ere London boasted a house."

The term "Lost Villages" has become common parlance for any village that has been abandoned. It is in many respects an unfortunate term, for nothing is lost in its entirety. The fact that it may be remembered in name only ensures its preservation.

Deserted is a more apt term but is less evocative. The term "lost" evokes an air of romance and mystery, whereas "deserted" sounds almost immoral. Yet, the reasons for abandonment were often immoral by definition, people being dispossessed of their homes for reasons of increasing the wealth of ruthless landlords, or for inundation to provide us with more water for us to waste.

Natural causes were the cause of many desertions. Climatic change and pestilence are understandable but genocide is unacceptable.

What has genocide to do with Derbyshire, you may ask? It is difficult to believe and is little recorded that genocide on a massive scale was once practised in England, on a scale in proportion to match the "ethnic cleansing" undertaken by Nazi Germany this century.

Of all the causes for village desertion, Derbyshire has them all bar one, coastal erosion, for whilst the county boasts most natural features in rich abundance, it does not have a border with the sea.

When discussing deserted villages we must also consider the villages which after desertion were repopulated, sometimes on the same site, at other times relocated on a nearby site.

Also, we are faced with the difficulty of definitions. What is or was a village? Most people accept that a community must boast a church and a pub to claim the right to village status. We must recall the early days when churches and pubs were not invented. What of the settlements of pre-history so abundant in the county, were these not villages? Many people dwelt in small settlements which we often call hamlets, out of necessity to give access to the land in the days when transport was rare and difficult to achieve.

As the number of deserted villages are not known and there is much research to be done in this, we cannot record them all. It runs into hundreds, and countrywide it runs into thousands. This book includes those lost communities which did not boast a church and therefore were not a parish in their own right - Willersley being a good example

This book will look at the Derbyshire Lost Villages by taking typical examples. It does not pretend to list them all for space does not permit this and we have yet to establish a finite list.

The stories which unfold are fascinating and it is well to remember that these villages were occupied by our ancestors. They had to work hard in mostly agrarian and mining cultures, living in hovels that we would not let our dogs occupy, with a life expectancy less than half of ours.

The problems facing the researcher into lost villages is determining when they were deserted and the reasons for the desertions.

This book will examine the following:

- mythical accounts
- villages of prehistory
- Roman settlements
- genocide
- climatic changes
- pestilence
- monastic clearances
- sheep clearances
- not in my back yard, often quoted as the NIMBY syndrome
- inundation
- urban sprawl

You are encouraged to search for examples yourselves, it is a surprisingly interesting and enjoyable way to have a day out, but PLEASE observe the country code and rights of way. Many deserted village sites are on private land.

Much research can be done at home during the winter months from maps and books in your own library. A rich source of information are the Ordnance Survey maps which cover the county. The White Peak and Dark Peak maps are especially useful being to a scale of 1:25000. These along with the 1:50000 series show some deserted villages but only a very few and given the scale of the villages lost one wonders why they chose the few they did.

For example by reference to the White Peak map at Grid Reference SK208657 can be seen, just north of Conksbury "Medieval Village (Site Of)". This is one of many in that area. Another means of recognising a deserted village is by looking at the civil parish names and trying to match village names to them. For example by reference to the Sheet 119 map, Grid Reference SK195482 the civil parish of "Offcote and Underwood" is given, but the only evidence of these villages to be found on the map are dwellings: Offcote Grange at SK204480 (there is an Offcote House nearby) and Underwood Farm at SK197484. This suggests the possibility of lost villages once having these names now remembered by surviving dwellings or dwellings built on pre-existing similarly named buildings.

A further rich source of information are nineteenth century trade directories and the Victoria County History which invariably give a potted history of each village in their texts. These frequently refer to the civil parish names and the condition of the villages.

Currently there is an excellent exhibition at Derby Museum on the Wardwick which deals with a deserted village under excavation at Barton Blount, of which more later. Roystone Grange has been partly excavated also.

CHAPTER TWO

MYTHICAL ACCOUNTS

Every county has its list of mythical villages, especially coastal counties whose locals will swear to having heard the church bells of a drowned community when fishing at sea.This is a common myth in the coastal villages of Lincolnshire and Cardigan Bay. Such stories can safely be dismissed but what of the mythical villages inland.

The most famous one in Derbyshire is Leash Fen, of which it is said

"When Chesterfield was heath and broom,
Leash Fen was a market town.
Now Leash Fen is all heath and broom,
and Chesterfield a Market town."

This is a long held tradition in the Chesterfield - Chatsworth area and Leash Fen bears some inspection.

The name Leash Fen features on the Ordnance Survey map in the square SK2973 and has all the attributes of prehistoric settlement. The location is typical at 280 metres ASL, it has a good water supply from Blake Brook and Blackleach Brook and the White Peak map indicates cairns, tumuli and an ancient field system nearby.

Which came first Leach or Leash? If the former it suggests the percolating of water, if the former it suggests hawking. Both might apply except that the word Fen suggests a link with water. However, there is no evidence that the area is or was a fen. Boggy it is and probably always has been but the word fen is rare in Derbyshire generally and unknown on these uplands. It is a word that more usually applies to low lying wetlands as found in East Anglia and Lincolnshire. Cranberries are found in abundance on these moors and fenberry is an alternative name for this fruiting sub-shrub.

The romantic in us would prefer to imagine that the area once boasted

8

a large and seemingly prosperous town of which little evidence remains today. It would be unusual in the extreme if this moor did not boast a lost prehistoric village, most of the moors in the area do but with more recognisable remains. Had Leash Fen existed and been of some substance, one would reasonably expect substantial remains such as hut circles to be evident. They are not. We must therefore consign this mythical town to the imagination rather than to the memory and accept that it probably never existed, that is until we have proof of its existence.

Before dismissing this myth as a myth, why are there three "crosses" in the area? Wibbersley Cross at SK294727 and another two at SK295748 (Bole Hill) and SK295753 nearby. These headless "crosses" are more likely to be megaliths which one would associate with a stone age settlement.

The residents of Bonsall speak convincingly of a lost village on Bonsall Leys and they will tell you of its name; Dunsley. No such name appears in the Domesday Book so what evidence do we have? A Dunsley Spring, emanating from a disused lead mine known as Dunsley Level, overlooks Marl Cottage at SK269569. This spring is a water supply for both Marl Cottage and Ible and is of very hard water, such that below it is a bank of tufa, a petrified stone, which the Victorians quarried to supply their gardens. Marl Cottage, a one time gamekeeper's cottage, is built of tufa; the naming of it as Marl Cottage is a mystery.

There is a recognisable Roman field system on Bonsall Leys centred on grid reference SK265572, the area having been heavily mined for lead and later tributed for fluorspar. Tradition has it that nearby Middleton-by-Wirksworth was a Roman penal colony. If this be true did they work both the mines and the fields? Is this how we have the tradition of the mythical lost village? If so why the name Dunsley?

Perhaps the answer lies in the Domesday Book. A village named Werredune is listed in the same hundred as Dunsley, the Hundred of Wirksworth, and its location has always been a mystery. The dun or dune in both names is common and it boasted six villagers having one plough and two bovates of land taxable. It also had an acre of meadow as well as underwood. All this would fit well with the site.

The location near to Dunsley Spring would have been ideal for a settlement, abundant water, a loamy soil, abundant wood and access to good roads; Hereward Street ran nearby through Wirksworth and Cromford on its way from Rocester via Ashbourne to Chesterfield.

If this be true, why should it have failed as a community? Possibly because of the depredations of lead mining taking up all the land, and climatic change, for it would have been a marginal village.

There is a similar tradition that Bradwell too was a Roman penal settlement, where the convicts served their sentences working the mines.

There are several other mythical sites scattered throughout the county. One reason for this tradition is probably based in the prehistoric sites so abundant in the Peak. Memories die hard in the county and the Celtic tradition is strong in the Peak District, where the traditions are still practised every year with well dressings and the Castleton Garlanding ceremony, Maidens Crantzes in Matlock and Ashford Churches, etc.

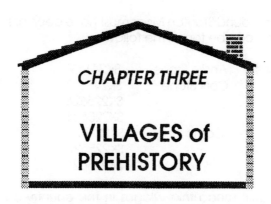

CHAPTER THREE

VILLAGES of PREHISTORY

"And see you the marks that show and fade
Like shadows on the Down
O they are the lines the Flint Men made,
To guard their wondrous towns."

Whilst there is much doubt surrounding the validity of Leash Fen, there are no such doubts about many prehistoric sites in the county.

Derbyshire is justifiably famous for such, second only to Wiltshire. The county boasts numerous stone circles, including the Stonehenge of the north, Arbor Low at SK160636. This is a fine recumbent henge of limestone liths, with embankments; a good barrow is adjacent and a mound is nearby called Gib Hill. The low is Neolithic (3500-2000BC), the barrow is later being of the Bronze Age (1800-800BC).

There is not space in this book to discuss the fascination of the circles and standing stones in the county, mostly in the Peak District, sufficient that we take them as an indicator of the activity that took place in the area in the millennia before the Romans came.

Early settlements are not difficult to find, and one outstanding and accessible example is the Bronze Age village and necropolis to be found on Stanton Moor. Apart from a superb henge called the "Nine Ladies", SK249635, there are immediately to the south of this circle numerous hut circles which denote a settlement of some size. This site together with another at Barbrook SK272782, "Lady's Cross" on the White Peak map, offered the peoples of the Bronze Age large cemetery sites. The one at Barbrook boasts at least seventy burial cairns.

The whole area around Stanton Moor must have been of some importance as nearby can be found the following:

- standing stones:	Andle Stone	SK241630
	Cork Stone	SK245627
		SK225626
- earthwork:		SK225624
	Castle Ring	SK221628
- stone circles:		SK225627
		SK238628

One of the largest megalithic villages in the country can be found stretching along the banks of the River Dove from the "Motte and Baileys" at SK113638 southeast to another motte at SK126615 and nearby earthworks at SK125610. The site includes Lud Well at SK124623 which was "waste" in Domesday, Lud is a name with strong Celtic connotations.

Another Bronze Age settlement can be seen on Gardom's Edge in the square SK2773 being one of many on the Edges. This one boasts a number of hut circles and a field system. It is adjacent to Leash Fen which we came across in chapter two. There is evidence that these people occupied this site from 2000BC to 1200BC when they abandoned it, probably due to overgrazing with the consequent soil erosion and climatic change. Its nearness to the mythical Leash Fen encourages us to wonder if the two are synonymous?

Iron Age settlements are well represented in the county and it was these settlements that the Romans encountered when they Invaded Britain in AD43, arriving in Derbyshire a few years later. These settlements would have survived this invasion for the Romans preferred to work with or enslave the cultures they found to their greater profit. It is from these people that the county inherits much of its Celtic folklore, for there is no other county so rich in such and already referred to.

An excellent lowland example of one of these settlements has been excavated at Willington, by the River Trent in the south of the county. The Rivers Trent and Dove boast many such lost villages which comprise farmsteads and field systems. The former were large round houses of wattle and daub with a conical thatched roof. At Willington these people grew wheat and barley and raised sheep, pigs, goats and oxen.

In the north of the county a hill fort and village of this period is slowly being eroded away on Mam Tor SK128937. The fort probably provided a safe refuge for the local farmers for tribal warfare was the norm during this period.

The remarks in the introduction concerning access should be well noted here. Whilst Stanton Moor and Mam Tor are easy of access, the other sites referred to are on private land and there is no public right of way. The Motte and Bailey at SK113638, known as Pilsbury Castle Rings, is to the side of a public right of way from Pilsbury to Crowdecote. A public right of way crosses the Barbrook site on White Edge Moor.

Arbor Low has a car park nearby and access is by a small fee paid at the nearby farm.

The site at Mam Tor is accessible by the famous ridge walk from the road to Barber Booth from Castleton (the direct route in front of the "Shimmering Mountain" is closed due to subsidence) to Hollin's Cross. The fort sits at an altitude of 1695 feet ASL.

The excavations at Roystone Grange have revealed early settlements and this site will be looked at in chapter eight.

CHAPTER FOUR

ROMAN SETTLEMENTS

"And see you, after rain, the trace
Of mound and ditch and wall?
O that was a Legion's camping-place,
When Caesar sailed from Gaul."

As mentioned in the previous chapter, the Romans reached Derbyshire a few years after landing in AD43, probably about AD50. By AD71 they had built a fort at York. By AD80 they had established a frontier with Scotland.

They built their famous roads across the county, mostly on the routes of existing trackways and most of which can be followed today and established their own settlements. There were several of these, the most important in the county being Derventio near Derby now remembered by the suburb of Little Chester at SK353376. Derventio takes its name from the adjacent River Derwent a Celtic name.

The site of the settlement has now been built over by the urban sprawl of Derby, it would appear that no-one had the foresight to preserve the site for until the last century there was still much to see.

With their penchant for bathing they established a bath house at Buxton on the site of a Celtic place of worship dedicated to Arnametis, a Celtic water sprite. The Romans named it Aqua Arnametiae being one of only two places in the country bearing the name Aqua, the other being Aqua Sulis where the bathhouse still exists at Bath, Avon. This is significant, for the Romans chose the name Aqua for the only two places in Britain where thermal waters naturally occur. They used other places for bathing, some claims are spurious, but the water whilst warm was not thermal by definition, the bath house at Stoney Middleton being one

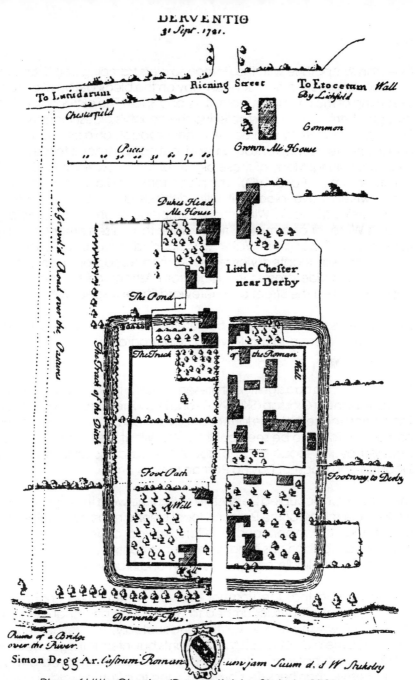

Plan of Little Chester (Derventio) by Stukely, 1721.
The site of the "Crown" is now occupied by the "Coach and Horses", the "Duke's Head" was removed by the railway. This map has east at the top. Note the reference to Lutudarum. "Ricning" Street is Ryknield Street.

such.

One can sympathise with the Roman soldiers tramping from Derventio to Aqua Arnametiae on a January day on the bleak Derbyshire moors, dreaming of their homes in warm Italy and Spain.The extraction of lead brought them here thus establishing the county's oldest industry apart from agriculture. They worked the mines probably on a tributing system and the numerous pigs of Roman lead that can be traced to the county verify the mining. Many of these pigs refer to the "silver works (EX ARG) at Lutudarum (LVT or LVTVD)". This place remained a mystery for many years, writers have placed it with dubious arguments variously at Chesterfield, Matlock, Wirksworth, Templeborough and incredibly - Church Wilne, or as a mining "field" rather than a settlement. Excavations before Carsington Water was flooded have established that Lutudarum was located where the Roman Road from Derventio to Aqua Arnametiae crosses the road from Ashbourne to Chesterfield, popularly called The Street and Hereward Street respectively. (SK2552)

The mystery is that this place is not referred to in the Antonine Itinerary there is a reference in the Ravenna Cosmography therefore it must have been of some importance.

The Romans also had significant presences at fortified sites at Melandra or Ardotalia near Glossop (SK009951) and Navio near Brough (SK182828). The former is accessible the latter is on private land. There are earthworks and a few stones to be seen but little else. What the Romans left were quarried by the locals and no doubt the buildings and walls in the localities can boast of having Roman hewn stones.

The tribe which occupied Derbyshire at this time were the Brigantes who worked the mines for the Romans, local chieftains being employed to ensure that the miners and smelters worked diligently. As already mentioned, tradition has it that penal settlements were established by the Romans at Middleton-by-Wirksworth and Bradwell.

The settlements that the Romans conquered remained unchanged except for those that succumbed to overgrazing and changes in the climate, of which we know little. Undoubtedly, the refinements of Imperial Rome did not touch the peasants but intermarriages were not unknown and many an attractive Brigante woman enjoyed a much better lifestyle than her sisters being married to a Roman soldier or if she were lucky a Roman landowner complete with Villa having running water, sanitation, central heating, plenty of food, good clothes, etc. Meanwhile the rest of the indigenous population lived much as they had before with the extra burden of paying tribute to Rome and having to work for new masters.

Uprisings were to no avail and were put down ruthlessly by the Roman soldiers. However, as the occupation grew older, the lot of the peasant did improve if only that he was prevented from warring with his neighbours.

The Romans suddenly left in about AD450, after being with us for four centuries. The indigenous Britons reverted to their old ways and depopulation must have taken place after tribal wars had taken their toll. From now on, until the Norman Conquest 600 years later Britain was invaded and populated by Scandinavians, Saxons and others each bringing new ideas and technologies. Intermarriage took place to create the polyglot mix that we are today.

We know little of the village life during this period but the village names were created and the early churches were founded, both recorded in the Domesday Book of 1086.

Any place name having Chester as part of it is Roman by definition. Outside the county we have nearby Manchester, Rocester, Doncaster and far away Chester. Within the county we have Chesterfield and Little Chester. The places having Brough as part of their placenames are also of Roman origin: nearby Templeborough and Brough itself. Most of these have been absorbed into modern towns and cities and their remains lie under our feet as we do our shopping.

Other smaller settlements existed at Brough or Navio or Anavio (SK182828) where an embankment and a few stones can still be seen. The footpath from the modern settlement of Brough to Hope passes through the site. Significantly Anavio is close to Bradwell, the supposed penal colony. The Roman road of Batham Gate also passes close by. There is a suggestion of a Bath House at SK174820, featured on the Dark Peak map as "The Bath".

There is little doubt that some of the buildings in the more modern Brough have stones quarried from Navio.

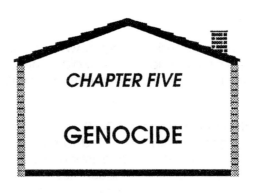

CHAPTER FIVE

GENOCIDE

One cannot write a history about any county without referring to that remarkable survey, the Domesday Book. It has already been mentioned but it deserves a chapter to itself. This book is not intended as a treatise on the Domesday Book but it will look at a period in our history little known about in the context of genocide on a grand scale.

William the Conqueror if you feared him or William the Bastard if you did not, became William I of England after his conquest of 1066. Twenty years later he caused this remarkable inventory to be made. The phrase within this which concerns us is "Wasta Est" (it is a waste).

There are many villages so annotated which in 1066 were paying taxes, for William wanted to know the taxability of each village in both 1066 and 1086 to see why his revenues had fallen. He had only himself to blame.

Space does not permit a full listing of every village that was fully or partly wasted but the following are representative and have been selected at random:

Village Name	Tax paid in 1066		Situation in 1086
Totally Waste			
Harthill	5s 4d	(0.265)	Waste
Hartington	40 shillings	(£2.00)	Waste
Linton	20 shillings	(£1.00)	Waste
Longstone	30 shillings	(£1.50)	Waste
Walton	20 shillings	(£1.00)	Waste

Devaluations

Barrow (upon Trent)	13s 4d	(£0.665)	Waste and 2s (10p)
Donisthorpe	5 shillings	(£0.25)	Waste and 12p (5p)
Killamarsh ·	16d	(£0.075)	Waste and 12d (5p)
Oakthorpe	5 shillings	(£0.25)	Waste and 4d (2p)
Ravenstone	15 shillings	(£0.75)	Waste and 12s (60p)
Thringstone	5 shillings	(£0.25)	Waste and 2d (1p)

The most telling entry is for Longdendale and Thornsett (near to Glossop) which together with several outliers paid 40 shillings (£2.00) in 1066 but by 1086 was "waste; woodland, unpastured, fit for hunting, the whole 8 leagues long and 4 leagues wide". A league was 1.5 miles, therefore the area in question was 72 square miles or 18,650 hectares.

Derby did not escape for the number of Burgesses dropped from 243 to 100, the number of mills fell from 14 to 10 and there were 103 residences which paid taxes in 1066 and were unoccupied in 1086.

So what happened?

William's conquest was not without its opponents especially the Northumbrians and the Welsh. The Northumbrians killed two of William's knights whilst trying to take possession of their new domains. An uprising followed which should have been supported by the Scots and the Danes who failed to materialise. William marched north in 1069 to put down the rebellion, meeting King Sweyn and his Danish army near the Humber. Having got rid of this nuisance he marched angrily north destroying everything in his path. His knights also took revenge in their own domains.

Between 1069 and 1071 the north was systematically destroyed. Not only did they put the villages and crops to the torch, they killed anything that moved. The slaughter of civilians was on a scale never seen before and not to be equalled until Nazi Germany in the World War 11. A chronicler rode with the Normans and he recorded that over 100,000 people were put to the sword, something like a tenth of the population. This chronicler, Orderic Vitalis, recorded, "It was terrible to see rotting corpses covered in multitudes of worms in the silent dwellings and deserted streets and roads with the atmosphere made foul by the stench of putrefaction. Nothing moved in the scorched ruins of the villages but the packs of wolves and wild dogs which tore apart the human corpses." After William left, the Scots came south and plundered what little was left and took the survivors, mostly women and children, into slavery. It is said that the survivors were happy to accept capture by the Scots to avoid starvation.

Thus in one evil stroke, England was depopulated. As this meant that there were less people to tend the fields and raise the cattle it also meant that the taxes could not be paid, hence the massive devaluation that resulted. It was not only a wicked thing to do, it was foolish also.

The Normans loved their hunting and established forests for that purpose. It has been calculated that Derbyshire in 1086 was 26% forest. Anyone found trespassing in these hunting grounds or Friths would be put to death, wandering dogs lost their front paws. Depopulation of these areas also ensued and we had two such Friths in the county, Duffield and Peak Forest wherein we have Chapel-en-le-Frith a Norman name if ever there was one.

Whilst their march north was via York and Durham, they ventured off their route to engage in their orgy of destruction and must have included Derbyshire in their itinerary, for there can be no other reason for the depopulation and devaluation in the county. Plague would not account for it for disease did not spread so rapidly in those times and now relatively unknown. Of the 351 villages recorded in the county, by 1086, 56 were waste and 103 were devalued by up to 75%. And this was fifteen years after the harrying took place, so the scars went deep. A few maintained their value and a very few increased their value, probably through the collectivisation of the remnant population coupled with good husbandry by wiser landlords. Most of the losses were close to the River Trent, always an easy route into the Midlands and one taken by William to access the north, whether by land or water.

No wonder that William begged God's forgiveness for what he had done to the English when making his last confession on his death bed.

These are the people that many a family historian works hard at to try and prove descent. The Celts for all their ways were a better option for one's ancestry.

This atrocity must have set this country back by at least one hundred years and some historians argue that the effects can still be seen today.

The location of some villages in Domesday have never been satisfactorily located:

Hundred of the High Peak
Langley - near to Chatsworth itself a Lost Village see Chapter10.
Muchedeswell - near to Wormhill?

Hundred of Wirksworth
Welledune - possibly Dunsley, see Chapter 2
Werredune - Warrington? Or could this be Wigwell. see Chapter 8

Hundred of Scarsdale
Greyhurst - Grassmoor near Chesterfield?
Padinc - Padleywood?
Ravensholm - linked with Upton in Domesday, see below.
Snodeswick
Tunstall - linked with Stainsby, Palterton and Scarcliffe in Domesday.
Upton - linked with Ravensholm in Domesday, see above.

Hundred of Repton
Bolun - is this connected with a smelting "Bole"?

Hundred of Morleyston
Cellesdene or Chelton - see Marsh below
Uluritune - follows Chelton in Domesday.

Some are remembered as place names without village communities:

Hundred of the High Peak
Thornsett - see this chapter.
Waterfield

Hundred of Wirksworth
Soham - between Glutton and Fernydale.

Hundred of Appletree
Bradley - now occupied by Belper.

Hundred of Morleystone
Smithycote - linked in Domesday with Codnor, Heanor andLangley.
Marsh - Marsh Flat Farm east of Chellaston at SK395305, a possible repopulation. Domesday lists Marsh with Chelton, could the latter be Chellaston? The mystery here is that Chellaston is separately listed.

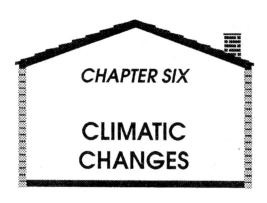

CHAPTER SIX

CLIMATIC CHANGES

We can protect our homes today against climatic change but we cannot protect our land.

Some land is notorious for being "cold", possibly the site of a frost hollow or a hillside exposed to the north. Such sites would be especially vulnerable to decay and this would lead to abandonment by the villagers who were dependent on the crops and grazing these lands provided. A token of such places lies in their very names, those having the word "cold" as a prefix or contained within it.

One example in the county is Coldeaton at SK148567 an excellent candidate for loss due to climatic change. This village had a high tax quota in 1334. A large green in front of two farms, Coldeaton Farm and Dove Top Farm, indicates a hut circle.

There were no doubt other losses due to climatic change, but this is a grey area as it is difficult to apportion reasons for depopulation. One can assume loss through changes in the climate when the real reason might be pestilence or granging.

We cannot appreciate when living in the twentieth century, the effect of climatic change when living off the land was precarious and the village economy being so dependent on the produce of the land. As recently as 1851, half of the population of England lived and depended on the land. Prior to that date we were an agrarian culture.

Hungry Bentley at SK180388 is another candidate for this category the name "Hungry" is evocative of a community that had to struggle on poor or hungry land. Hungry or hungrig is old English for poor or unproductive land. This suggests overgrazing on already poor land, possibly due to erosion from the effects of continual wet seasons over several years. This site, which lies mostly in a field called Brookfields, lies immediately southwest of Bentley Fields Farm and has a clearly definable set of streets. With great foresight, the owners of this farm provide access to the site as part of their Open Farm system and access can be arranged through them but not otherwise.

Near to this site lie the lost villages of Alkmonton, Sapperton, Bupton and Ash together with Longford and Barton Blount. These latter two will be dealt with in chapter ten.

Alkmonton at SK196386 may have suffered a similar fate to Hungry Bentley, the migration of its population. It paid a large tax quota in 1334 of 22s 6d (£1.125). A large field which can be viewed from the Longford to Yeaveley road has remains of streets and houses in the ground. The Norman font which resides in the new church at the new Alkmonton, a nearby hamlet at SK187386, came from the original Alkmonton now remembered by Alkmonton Old Hall at SK194373 with a nearby moated site. Curiously, the Roman road of Long Lane was diverted round Alkmonton as it was round adjoining Longford. The latter is explained by emparkment but the former may be an indication of the importance of the village. The chapel which once stood in the old village is the supposed resting place of St Alkmund when his corpse was being conveyed to Derby, where a shrine was created to him. His sarcophagus can be seen in Derby Museum. A "Chapel" is marked on the 6" map of the area in a field called Cockshut Close, adjacent to today's Hall Farm. The new village might be the resettled old village.

In 1849 the Township of Alkmonton and the Liberty of Hungry Bentley were formed into a parish called the Chapelry District of Alkmonton. Lord Vernon was the Lord of the Manor and owner of the liberty of 1074 acres. In the census of 1891 it had a population of only 77.

Sapperton at SK186345 and Ash at SK261325 were also abandoned for the same reason as was Bupton at SK224374, Sapperton is remembered by a manor on the site, Bupton by a hamlet of the same name and Ash by Ashe Hall on the site. There is nothing to be seen of these lost villages apart from some mounds in a field at Bupton Corner (SK224374). There is a possibility that Bupton was a victim of the sheep clearances, see chapter nine.

Whilst all these villages were devalued in 1086, they were far from being worthless, indeed Bupton paid £11.00 in taxes to three Lords

Chunal, now a few cottages on the western edge of Kinder at SK034917 was waste at the time of Domesday and it never recovered, possibly due to its location on marginal land.

The temptation to overgraze an area of land must have been great to our ancestors and it would have taken only a moderate change in the weather for the worse over a succession of seasons to cause a village to fail. This would be particularly true of the marginal villages which were situated on the edges of the moorland areas. If lead mining could not sustain them, the land certainly could not in some instances. The economy of many of these villages depended on a curious mix of mining and farming. The former in the summer when the water tables were low to permit access to the mines, the latter in spring when the cattle and sheep had to be grazed and in autumn when the harvest had to be gathered. A slump in the price of lead could aggravate this delicate economy but this coupled with poor weather could be catastrophic.

A visit by the plague would then spell total disaster to an already weak and undernourished community.

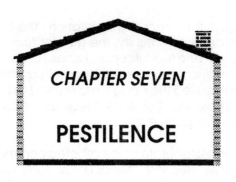

CHAPTER SEVEN

PESTILENCE

"Ring a ring o'roses,
Our pockets full of posies,
A'tishoo, a'tishoo,
We all fall down."

We all sang this nursery rhyme in our childhood and children still do so today. It recalls the great plagues which beset this country at frequent intervals from 1348 to 1665. The Great Pestilence, which caused the most damage was from 1348 to 1350.

The 'ring o'roses' was the first manifestation of the disease on the skin, the posies of flowers were believed to ward off the plague - witness the Judges who still carry posies to court in London - and those about to die of the plague would smell sweet flowers, they would then sneeze and promptly die. The tragic story of the Derbyshire plague village of Eyam has been told many times elsewhere, but one recalls the gallant Revd William Mompesson remarking that Catherine his wife and helpmate, through this traumatic period one day could smell sweet flowers, he and she both knew that she was as good as a dead woman.

The plague in question was the bubonic plague, the black death (the skin turned black) or in common parlance of the times, the Pestilence. The visitation to these shores originated in Kaffa on the Crimea when under siege by the Tartars. They catapulted infected corpses into the city. In 1347, the ships which supplied this city with provisions brought the disease back to Messina, Sicily.

From then on it advanced unchecked throughout Europe causing devastation on a huge scale. It arrived in England by trading vessels visiting the south coast ports arriving in London in 1348. It was quickly carried throughout the land by itinerant workers, drovers and pack men.

We cannot imagine the horror of this visitation - the constant fear that it would arrive in one's community, the greater fear that it would visit one's own family, and the fearful consequences of catching this virulent and incurable condition. It was a quack doctor's and medicine maker's dream. Those who buried the dead were entitled to the possessions of the deceased as payment. Some were fearless or poor enough to take this highly risky and gruesome job.

The Bishop of Winchester wrote of the afflicted communities, *"Every joy has ceased in them, pleasant sounds are hushed, and every note of gladness is vanished. They have become abodes of horror, ..."*

The plague is carried by rat fleas, and it arrived in Eyam in a bale of old clothes imported from London. Graves of plague victims can be seen in a field at Eyam called the Rye Ley, hence the Riley Graves. These have been assembled in the centre of the field and walled and are of the Hancock family, who survive in the area to today, and it is said that the entire family was buried by the wife of one and the mother of the remainder. These graves can be found at SK225767 and are in the care of the National Trust and are accessible at any time.

The burial sites of plague victims can be found by road names, such as:

- Blagreaves Lane, Littleover (Blagreaves = Black Graves)
- Lousygreaves Lane, Spondon (Lousy = lice or flea infested)

It is difficult to determine which villages became depopulated due to disease as opposed to sheep clearances. It was often convenient for land owners to blame the pestilence when the truth was their own selfish motives to grow more wool.

It is reasonable to assume that the valley villages are better candidates for sheep clearances and the upland villages were victims of the plague. However, the issue is confusing without hard evidence but some suggested depopulation due to the Pestilence are offered as follows:

- Lea at SK 195517 near to Tissington and just south of Lea Hall, the Civil Parish is called Lea Hall.

- Underwood at SK197484 and Offcote at SK204480 near to Ashbourne are both likely candidates although the fact that Offcote is now occupied by Offcote Grange may suggest a monastic clearance. This does not preclude it from loss by plague, as a grange did not exist here, it was possibly the location of a monastic village having links with a grange, occupied by peasant workers who may have had a grange barn or granary. The Civil Parish is shown as Offcote and Underwood. The possibility of a lost village of Sturston at SK202467 nearby suggests a plague village. Sturston must have been of some importance at one time as the main road in Ashbourne which goes to Belper, once a turnpike, is named Sturston Lane. Sturston once boasted its own hall which dated from the 12th century, now also lost.

- Compton, a highway in Ashbourne is another possibility. The road south of the brook is called the Compton and the Civil Parish is Clifton and Compton. The writer believes that the rivalry between the "Uppards" and the "Downards" when battling it out with the Ashbourne Shrovetide Ball Game is the Celtic game between the two communities of Ashbourne and Compton. The remnants of a village called Compton would naturally absorb into the town of Ashbourne. The buildings which now form Compton are mostly the Victorian urban sprawl surrounding a mill, with the notable exception of the Georgian House, once the town house of the Beresfords, now occupied by Lloyds' bank.

People deserting a town for the country to escape the pestilence, 1630.

CHAPTER EIGHT

MONASTIC CLEARANCES

"Trackway and Camp and City lost,
Salt Marsh where now is corn -
Old Wars, old peace, old Arts that cease,
And so was England born!"

It seems inhuman and immoral that a religion which preaches brotherly love and charity should create a system which dispossessed the poor from their homes and livelihood.

Before the dissolution the church held huge tracts of land, and much of this land was farmed by monastic granges. Derbyshire had numerous of these with lands which covered large areas of the county.

This situation existed at Domesday but these lands were added to by the landowners, a method of buying mercy and in the hope that such bequests would ensure forgiveness for past sins on the day of judgement. As a consequence the monasteries grew rich out of these lands which they farmed using local paid labour. However, they did not like the villagers living on this land and they were often dispossessed.

The county has numerous instances of this and the following list is not exhaustive:

Mother House	Granges	Lost Villages
Buildwas Abbey (Cistercian)	Ivonbrook	SK245585
	Where once stood Ible Manor House the site now occupied by Wigley Meadow Farm.	
Beauchief Abbey (Premonstratensian)	Harewood	SK312680

Little Chester, near Derby, the Roman Derventio.
The terraced housing covers much of this important site but there
is evidence of a field system in Chester Green at the bottom and in
the field at the top. Comparison with Stukeley's plan which follows is
interesting. If the reader identifies the "Coach and Horses" at the
south west corner of the obvious cross-road centre right (originally
the "Crown" and the river running across the north west corner, some
idea of the position and extent of the Roman settlement can be
had. The Roman road which crossed the river is still evident
by a track way middle left.
(CUC reference CBK 27 reproduced with permission)

An aerial view of Barton Blount which is similar to Hungry Bentley taken in December, 1966 in many respects. Note the hoolow way, house platforms and lynchets. The large filed to the west is heavily ploughed and hides part of the village.
(CUC reference: AQI 48 reproduced with permission)

Site of Roystone Grange - 1999. Photo - John N. Merrill.

Part of Ashopton village wh
Looking north-west, 5th Ma
ished and the ruins are nov
over this viaduct not rea
(Severn Trent Wa

viaduct was under construction.
941. These buildings were demol-
r water. How many people drive
what once lay beneath them?
lection, with permission)

Present day Roystone Grange. Photo - John N. Merrill.

Chapel like building - Pump House for the former Cromford and High Peak Railway - plaque on right of building about Roystone Grange. Photo - John N. Merrill

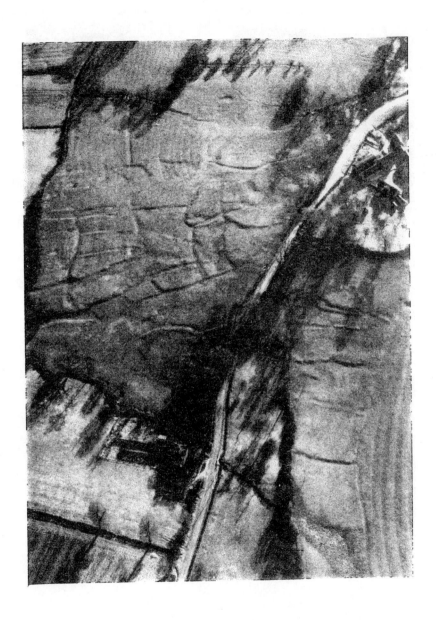

An aerial view of Osleston with old field boundaries and
house platforms in abundance. Taken in February, 1969
(CUC reference: AWW 47 reproduced with permission)

An aerial view of Hungry Bentley taken in December, 1966
A hollow way can be seen running from the farmhouse south
and turning west. House platforms can be seen either side of this way
and at the bottom medieval lynchets and croft boundaries.
(CUC reference: AQl 33 reproduced with permission)

Burton Abbey (Benedictine)	Hanson Grange This featured in Domesday as waste and is near to Cold Eaton see Chapter 6.	SK152545
Dale Abbey (Premonstratensian)	Griffe	SK253564
Darley Abbey (Augustinian)	Scarcliffe This featured in Domesday with a value of £2.50 together with Palterton and Tunstall.	SK500701
	Wessington This also features in Domesday with a reduced value.	SK370570?
	Wigwell	SK305544
	Aldwark Now a village with humps in the "Green" which suggest an earlier settlement.	SK231582
Dunstable Priory (Augustinian)	Mouldridge	SK202594
	Bradbourne With a value of £1.50 in Domesday reduced from £2.00.	SK210525
Garendon Abbey (Cistercian)	Roystone	SK201568
	Heathcote	SK1460
	Biggin	SK147590
Leicester Abbey (Augustinian)	Meadow Place	SK201658
	Middleton	SK1963
Newstead Priory (Augustinian)	Hardwick	See Chapter Ten
Roche Abbey (Cistercian)	One Ash Grange	SK169653
Rufford Abbey (Cistercian)	Abney Waste in Domesday	SK191787

In fairness to the monks, they were good husbandmen and their lands were well kept. The produce was for feeding the Grange and the mother house, the surplus was sold.

It is worthy of note that the mother houses were not always within the county. Beauchief was in Yorkshire close to Sheffield, therefore not too far away, Roche also was in Yorkshire, Newstead is in Nottinghamshire close to Mansfield, to become the home of Lord Byron, Rufford also was in Nottinghamshire, the site becoming a fine country house, Leicester Abbey was in the city of that name, Garendon in the county of that name and further away Dunstable in Bedfordshire.

The granges of Meadowplace and One Ash, the latter a penal grange for recalcitrant monks, are now occupied by farms. The depopulated villages nearby which were taken over by the brothers are:

- Conksbury, marked on the White Peak map as "Medieval Village - site of" at SK208657. This was near to Conksbury Bridge over the River Lathkill and lies to the west of Conksbury Hall, it is on private land and there is nothing to see.

- Harthill at SK229647, featured as Harthill Hall on the maps. There is a large and old barn at this farm, the occupants believing it to have been a chapel. It is more likely to have been a barn or granary. Some disturbed ground to the side of the farm suggests a lost village mixed with the remains of lead mining, such that it is difficult to determine the one from the other.

- Mouldridge, with the nearby lost village of Gratton at SK208618, Fishpond Wood nearby in Gratton Dale suggests monastic fish stews.

Wigwell Grange was viewed by the monks as a pleasant place to be sent to. No penance here, it was probably a welcome relief from the tedium of the mother house, the remnants of which can still be seen in the industrial hamlet of Darley Abbey, north of Derby at SK353383. These monks certainly worked the coal measures nearby using bell pits and there is evidence of peat cuttings in the vicinity. There is evidence of the original grange in the cellars of the current Wigwell Grange. One conjectures if this was the site of the lost Werredune mentioned in Domesday? Nearby at SK301543 is a moated site close to a megalith, with evidence of a village in the same field, so the area has been occupied for more than three millennia.

Roystone Grange has been part excavated. The original grange was quarried for the stone out of which the present 'grange' was built. During the reign of Henry II, one Adam of Harthill gave Revestones to the abbey. This was a 400 acre estate which by 1366 was producing and exporting wool to Europe. After the fourteenth century the site was leased and by 1535/6 the tenant was a Rowland Babington who operated it as a mixed farm using ox ploughs. From these labours we get the linchets which are evident in the vicinity. One wonders if it was this same Adam of Harthill who gave the Harthill site to the church?

Sheffield University have excavated part of the site and this can be visited. Thus far they have uncovered a bow shaped dairy building 17 m by 12 m, the north end of which was the dairy, a central room had a hearth for warming the milk and the south end was a parlour with an oven. So it is clear that the monks were making cheese.

The site is criss-crossed with drains to cope with the wetter years of the thirteenth and fourteenth centuries, the same climatic changes that depopulated many villages.

A building called the chapel was a building of more modern date which housed an air pump.

A Grange Barn at Steeple (Steep Hill) Grange, near Wirksworth, was demolished for its dressed stone by Arkwright, to contribute to the building of his first mill at Cromford.

Harthill Barn, possibly a grange barn, tastefully converted into holiday lets. Tradition has it that this was the monks' chapel but this is unlikely. (Photograph by the author.)

CHAPTER NINE

SHEEP CLEARANCES

Lead miners who died at their work in the lead mining "Fields" of the county were buried in a shroud of Derbyshire wool until 1852, everyone had to have a woollen shroud from 1666 until 1814 and a "Woolsack" is the official seat of the Lord Chancellor as Speaker of the House of Lords. Such was the importance of wool as a staple product in this country. English wool was much sought after across Europe and fortunes could be made out of it.

The landowners knowing this grazed sheep anywhere they could find grass including the high moors and the villages. This led to the depopulation of villages to make way for the sheep.

It is difficult to discriminate between villages lost to plague and those lost to sheep. The plague was often blamed to ease the conscience of the landowner. Generally the sheep clearances occurred in the valleys especially in the south of the county and the following are a few speculative sites:

- Bearwardcote at SK283334 west of the Pastures Hospital, Mickleover and once occupied by a moated house of circa 1100, demolished in 1790. The present Bearwoodcote Hall is of the last century.

- Hoon at SK224299 near to Hatton now occupied by Hoonhay is given as the location of the lost village by Beresford. A more likely location would have been Hoon Hall also now lost possibly at SK230316.

- Arleston at SK337297 on the banks of the Trent and Mersey Canal and nearby Sinfin at SK343312 and Potlock at SK313287 all close to the River Trent. Sinfin is now remembered as a suburb of Derby recently buried under urban sprawl. Arleston and Sinfin were linked for tax purposes. There is nothing to be seen at any of these sites apart from Arleston House, a sixteenth century farmhouse.

- Drakelow in the square SK2420 now buried under Drakelow Power Generating Station. Whilst this is south of Burton-upon- Trent, Staffordshire it lies in Derbyshire. It is regrettable that this ancient Celtic site should be so lost, for Drakelow means Dragon's Hill as does Wormhill further north in the Peak District.

- Ballidon at SK2054 has been quarried away. The present hamlet of Ballidon is a possible relocation.

- Birchill at SK216707 is represented by Birchills Farm.

- Bubnell at SK248725 has Bubnell Hall of the 17th century and a few cottages from repopulation.

- Callow at SK269518 is now a moated house called Callow Hall. Beresford suggests Callow Moor at SK263518.

- Cottons at SK3532 is of doubtful location but certainly buried under the ordnance works built this century, near to Sinfin.

- Cowley probably stood where Stanton Lees now stands at SK253632

- Priestcliffe at SK140720 once boasted a hall now long vanished.

- Shuckstonefield at SK3656 near to Wessington might have been a monastic clearance, no trace is available.

- Potter Somersall at SK143353 is remembered by Somersall House.

- Stoke at SK239769 (not SK2179 as suggested by Domesday) is represented by a hamlet and nearby Stoke Hall. This Stoke was a manor of Hope with which it is linked in Domesday.

- Uftonfields at SK397563 has Ufton Fields Farm.

- Eaton Dovedale at SK109373 and nearby Sedsall at SK111376, are represented by Eaton Dovedale Farm and a place name of Sedsall, now Doveridge Woodhouse which once boasted a Manor House now long lost.

- Farley at SK294623 is remembered by an area of Matlock and specifically by Farley Farm.

- Ingleby at SK350270 is now a riverside hamlet.

- Makeney at SK353447 is a hamlet having Makeney Old Hall of the late 16th century.

- Owlcotes at SK4467?

- Ashover moeities, split in 1203:

Eastwood; Hall of the 15th and 16th Centuries,
        now ruinous at SK358629

Overton; Hall dates from 1693-99, original house of 1323,
        at SK345623

Eddlestow: The present farmhouse was the barn for a hall
        now gone which date from the 16th and 17th
        Centuries, at SK328631

Of the above none were waste at the time of Domesday, indeed they were generally prosperous by the standards of that time.

CHAPER TEN

THE NIMBY
SYNDROME

"NIMBY" is a facetious acronym for "Not in my Back Yard" an expression which is particularly apt in this instance.

Derbyshire is blessed with some very fine country houses, the larger ones being built on sites chosen for reasons of availability of materials, water supply, access to the owner's estates, a terrain which lent itself to landscaping and fine outlooks. This last reason was often marred by the unwelcome view of an unsightly village with even more unsightly peasants, a constant reminder to the land owner how his workers and servants lived.

Our finest country house is generally agreed to be Chatsworth House, itself built on the site of Chatsworth Village SK2670 which was originally a monastic grange or barn. When the house was extended by the 6th Duke of Devonshire, the original village of Edensor came into view from the west front together with its manor house, the original dating from 1241, coming into the possession of the Cavendishes in the 17th Century. He caused this village to be relocated to its present site, and in so doing created a model village second to none in the country. The new village of Edensor is well worth studying for its unique mixture of architectural styles. The original village existed up to 1838 and traces of it can be seen in the parkland grass where the access road to the house joins the road from Rowsley to Baslow (B6012), in the crook of the bend almost opposite Naboth's Vineyard at SK253698. A moated site at SK257702 could have been the original Chatsworth Manor site. Calton at SK685245 once boasted a seat of the Calton family from the 14th Century, another clearance.

This is an instance where the villagers were relocated into better housing rather than being dispossessed. Another such instance is Sudbury which was also relocated by the builders of Sudbury Hall, Mary and later George Vernon. During the long process of building this fine Carolinian house, 1613 to 1670's, the village which stood in what is now the front

Naboth's vineyard, the last remnant of the original village of Edensor. The disturbed ground to the right is evidence of house platforms. Photograph by the author.

lawn was relocated into quality houses which now form the present village. The outline of the original Sudbury can be seen in the Autumn from the house roof.

Other villagers were not treated with the same benevolence or respect. There is a long list of villages destroyed by house builders to enable them to enjoy a pleasant prospect. These are sometimes recognisable by the existence of the church which was often left intact. The reasons for this are apparent: it created a place of worship for the house owner, it acted as a benevolence to the dispossessed parishioners and it was a garden ornament on a large scale. It was also probably the only building of any substance within the original village.

Oliver Goldsmith was inspired to write his poem "The Deserted Village"; and to quote only two lines:

> *"Along the lawn, where scatter'd hamlets rose.*
> *Unwieldy wealth, and cumbrous pomp repose."*

Goldsmith wrote this during the house building boom of the 18th century, his poem was dated 1770. He wrote in Lloyds Evening Post in June 1762, "I staid (sic) 'till the day on which they were compelled to remove ......their neat gardens and well cultivated fields were left to desolation.......I am informed that nothing is more common than such revolutions." He was staying at the time at Newnham Courtney Hall south of Oxford. A rose garden replaced the village bar one hovel occupied by an old crone, which was kept for some inexplicable reason, possibly as a garden ornament?

The disappearance of so many villages around Chesterfield was due to "the Earl of Leicester pulled down whole towns and villages for his pleasure". This was quoted in 1584. The towns referred to are probably the villages which now form part of the Borough of Chesterfield or are close by such as Whittington, Tapton, Brimington and Newbold. Most of these were repopulated later as part of the industrial expansion of Chesterfield. Boythorpe is now lost and exists as an area of Chesterfield only (SK3769), Greyhurst is also lost, featuring in Domesday, part of Hasland. Other possible village sites destroyed by the Earl are Dunston now known as Sheepbridge (SK365745), Holme (SK354724), Walton (359691) now built over in recent times, and Somersall (SK354699).

Earlier than this we have villages being destroyed to make way for large houses such as Haddon Hall; Nether Haddon at SK235664 and possibly Pickering at SK238658 now remembered as Pickery Corner, the junction of the B5056 and the A6 roads. The loss of nearby Burton at SK220677 was much later to make way for the gothic mansion named Burton Closes.

The best known such lost village is Barton Blount at SK209346 which was cleared to make way for the house. The church was retained but is now ruinous. This site has been partly excavated and a display about it can be seen in Derby Museum. Another lost village which has only its church as a reminder is Longford at SK215383. The villagers were relocated to a new Longford close to the lost village of Bupton. Unlike Barton Blount, this church is cherished and used. The builder of the part Tudor house destroyed not only the village but also diverted the Roman road, Long Lane, to circumvent his park.

A village which has been lost to industry is Osmaston-by-Derby which is now under the Osmaston Park Industrial Estate. The great house, church and village are now gone. The last to go was the church of St James-the-Less, pulled down as recently as 1951 when the churchyard was also cleared, the bodies being reinterred in a mass grave in the Nottingham Road Cemetery, Derby. In 1888 the then Midland Railway Company bought the house and estate from the Wilmot family for £90,000 to provide space for extra workshops. The house was used as offices, then as a golf club before falling into disrepair, being demolished in 1938. All that remains of this sad village is the grave of a Chinaman, Charles Osmaston, which is now safe in private ownership. The one mile long Grand Drive is now the tarmacadamed and treeless Ascot Drive. The church stood at SK369338.

St. James the Less, Osmaston-by-Derby now occupied by the Osmaston Park Industrial Estate. This was sadly demolished in 1951. This attractive little church along with the vicarage stood at the corner of Osmaston Park Road which was itself originally a mile long park drive.

Another two examples of Houses which retained the church are Foremark Hall of 1755, now a preparatory school for Repton School, at SK330265; Bretby Hall, now a hospital and the church rebuilt on its original site, at SK300225; Calke Abbey at SK369223 (church) and SK366227 (house, now National Trust). Calke Abbey is so called for it was built on the site of an Augustinian Priory founded circa 1130, the present house built in 1703 replaced the original one of 1621, retaining some of the walls of the original monastery.

Nearer to Derby we have Kedleston Hall complete with church, which occupies the site of the village of Kedleston at SK312403 and a second village which was destroyed, Ireton Parva at SK314415. The present Kedleston is an estate village of later date. Close by is the house of Meynell Langley at SK301398 but this is churchless.

There is an instance where a village was cleared and a church built. Sir Richard Arkwright caused Willersley Castle to be built on the north bank of the River Derwent at the bottom of Matlock Dale. He could not occupy it for it burnt down on completion and was not fit for habitation until after his death in 1792. His son completed the house and built the church which was consecrated in 1859 as both a place of worship and a mausoleum for the family. However, trapped between the cliff face and the river at SK298572 was the village of Willersley, a ramshackle collection of hovels built onto the rock face. The inhabitants were rehoused in the newly built industrial village of Cromford nearby, to remove the eyesore from the gaze of the family. The church of St Mary was built on the site of a lead smelter, kniown as the Green, tradition has it that a church stood on this site prior to the lead smelter. The power for which was from a wheel on the river, the village provided the labour.

Cromford is an excellent example of an early industrial village and most of Arkwright's houses remain. The original Cromford or Crumeford was removed along with most of a hamlet called Scarthin, commemorated today by Scarthin Promenade at SK295569. Some of the original cottages which formed part of Scarthin were demolished to make way for council flats in recent times. Cromford was not placed on the Derwent as commonly believed but on Bonsall Brook. The finest of the Arkwright houses can be seen on both sides of North Street with the school at its end built by the benefactor's son. Some cottages, particularly on Bedehouse Lane, are remnants of the original village.

Other such depopulations are:

- Elvaston at SK411325 and Thulston at SK414317 to make way for Elvaston Castle of 1633 for the Harrington family.

- Hazelbadge at SK171800 for Hazelbadge Hall 1549.

- Hopwell at SK440363 for Hopwell Hall now demolished.

- Houghpark in Domesday at SK241464, a moated site now called the Hough (a scheduled site), together with Upper Hulland having its church at SK249475 to make way for Hulland Hall of 1777 for the Borowe family; the Bradbourne family occupied the moated site from 1296 to 1594. The present Hulland Ward is a more recent settlement.

- Catton at SK207155, named Catton Hall built in 1741-2.

- Egstow at SK392649, named Egstow Hall built for the Hunloke family in the 17th century.

- Mapleton, Mappleton in Domesday and pronounced such today by the locals, is a repopulation from Okeover across the River Dove in Staffordshire where the church stands at SK158481 close to the hall of the same name.

Finally, we cannot let this chapter be completed without remembering that formidable woman and inveterate house builder, Elizabeth the Countess of Shrewsbury, or as we familiarly prefer her to be known, "Bess of Hardwick". She abandoned the part built Hardwick Old Hall and on the death of her fourth husband, the Earl of Shrewsbury, she started the Hardwick Hall that we know today. The death of her fourth husband left her the richest woman in England second only to Queen Elizabeth I. The site was originally occupied by an Augustinian grange belonging to Newstead Abbey in Nottinghamshire. The Hall stands on an elevated site at SK462637. She also caused several villages to be depopulated to create the park, Hardstoft at SK457633, badly devalued at Domesday and remembered by the Hardstoft Inn, and Ault Hucknall at SK467653 where the church exists and wherein is buried our greatest philosopher, Thomas Hobbes, who died at Hardwick in 1679 at the age of 91. Hardstoft was moved to its present location at SK440630. Stainsby at SK449656 and Tunstall, location unknown, are also likely candidates for clearance by Bess.

CHAPTER ELEVEN

INUNDATION

The drowning of villages is usually associated with erosion by the sea. In recent years we have witnessed the pictures on television of a hotel falling into the sea at Scarborough, North Yorkshire, due to the erosion of a cliff.

One cannot get further from the sea than Derbyshire, yet we have two drowned villages, Derwent and Ashopton, both named after the rivers which they spanned, the Derwent and the Ashop.

The ever increasing demand for water has caused us to drown valleys to create reservoirs. The water undertakings now prefer to call them waters, as in Carsington Water, to make them appear more user friendly. This does not disguise the fact that land and sometimes dwellings are drowned.

In the case of Carsington Water, the already lost Roman community of Lutudarum was drowned, but in the High Peak the creation of a series of reservoirs, starting with Howden Reservoir which overspills into Derwent Reservoir which overspills into Ladybower Reservoir, caused the inundation of two charming villages. Howden and Derwent were built in the years 1901 to 1912 and 1902 to 1916 respectively, Ladybower under whose waters the villages were inundated came later.

The village of Derwent lies under the Ladybower Reservoir at SK185885. During the drought of 1946 the village was exposed and sightseers explored the remains including the church tower. This latter was dynamited as it was a hazard at that time. Before this operation, the four bells were removed and stored at Chesterfield, one was recast and hung elsewhere. The church tower was all that was left standing before inundation started. During times of severe drought one can still wander round the roads and remains of the houses.

Derwent boasted a fine hall, a youth hostel just prior to its demolition, a one time residence of a younger son of the Duke of Norfolk who owned land in the area. Gateways to the hall drives can be seen at SK176893 and SK185887.

Ashopton stood underneath the present Ashopton Viaduct at SK194864. Its bridge remains under water at this spot where it crossed the River Ashop. This smaller community could not boast a hall but did provide the area with an inn and smithy.

The building of the Howden and Derwent dams caused a temporary village to be created, known as Tin Town locally but officially named Birchenlee, it was largely built of corrugated steel. It was a complete village in every sense and comprised a chapel, community hall and housing. It was built in the period 1901-02 being occupied, or partially occupied from 1901 to 1914, when it was demolished. This was cleared away when the work was finished, but many people boast of having been born in this temporary community. Whilst it existed for so short a time, it is an unique example of a village being built and deserted within a person's life span. Birchenlee stood at SK167915 and much evidence of it can be found amongst the trees, with clearly defined roads, the incinerator and the stone foundations of some of the houses.

The Ladybower scheme took eleven years to build and was opened on 25th September 1945 by HM King George VI.

All that remains to be seen of these villages is the old packhorse bridge re-erected on the same route that it served and over the same river which it crossed but closer to its source at Slippery Stones at SK169951. The bridge was photographed, dismantled, the stones numbered and stored throughout the Second World War, being re-erected at the expense of the Council for the Preservation of Rural England as a memorial to a John Derry, a journalist and writer of Sheffield. The stone pillars which stood at the gate to Derwent Hall were redressed and re-erected at the gates of Ladybower Dam. The Derwent village war memorial was re-erected overlooking the spot where it originally stood (SK182884), the interred were exhumed from Derwent churchyard and reinterred in Bamford churchyard.

Opinions differ about the morality of this undertaking. Two villages and many farms together with beautiful dales have been lost. Other farms had to be abandoned due to the decrease in farmable land, these are now either ruinous or used for other purposes. Others will point to the benefits of ample water for the cities of Derby, Nottingham and Leicester. No-one can deny that these lakes together with the recently planted woodlands are a great asset to the angler, walker and tripper. Derbyshire now has a Lake District.

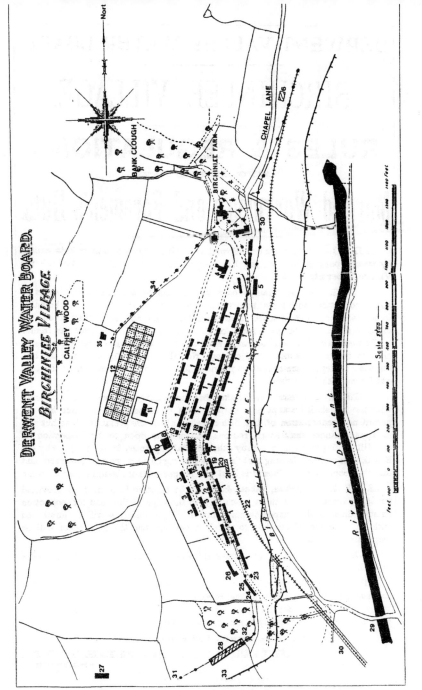

Plan of Birchenlee Village better known as Tin Town. This was a temporary village for the workers and their families whilst working on the Derwent and Howden dams. The key tells us what the various huts were used for. (Severn Trent Water Collection).

DERWENT VALLEY WATER BOARD.

BIRCHINLEE VILLAGE.

RULES & REGULATIONS
RELATIVE TO

Married Workmen's and Foremen's Huts.

RULE 1.--Tenants are not allowed to receive lodgers into their huts except by special permission from the Engineer obtained on application through the Village Superintendent.

RULE 2.--The only lamps permitted in the huts to be safety lamps of approved pattern with metal reservoirs. Any lamps not approved will be liable to confiscation if not removed from the hut after due notice has been given. In the case of hanging lamps a metal or glass bell must be hung over the funnel. The wooden ceiling over the lamps shall be protected by sheet iron, space being allowed between the plate and ceiling. No oil shall be stored within the hut, but shall be kept in the coal store provided for each hut. Petroleum of the best quality only shall be used.

RULE 3.--The tenant undertakes that the sanitary arrangements connected with the hut shall be kept in a perfect state of cleanliness and that he will permit no accumulation of dirt, filth or refuse about the premises. The hut and its appurtenances shall at all reasonable times be open to the inspection of the Village Superintendent or any other official appointed for the purpose by the Board, with a view of seeing that the rules and regulations are duly observed, and that the property of the Board is kept in a proper state of cleanliness and repair.

RULE 4.--All refuse, ashes, &c. must be emptied into the bins provided for the purpose which must be carried to the edge of the road for collection on such days as the Inspector may appoint. Each dust-bin will be numbered with the number of the hut to which it belongs, and the hut-keeper will be responsible for the same.

RULE 5.--A copy of the above rules shall be posted in the living room of each hut.

RULE 6.--The above rules may at any time be added to or varied by the Board. Infringement of any of the above rules or any other rules hereafter made will render the offender liable to notice to quit, and a second offence after warning will be followed by summary ejectment.

By order of the Derwent Valley Water Board.

EDWARD SANDEMAN,
ENGINEER.

*The rules and regulations imposed by the Derwent Valley Water Board on the occupants of the huts.
(Severn Trent Water Collection).*

CHAPTER TWELVE

URBAN SPRAWL

Urban sprawl cannot be criticised as a phenomenon, it is a consequence of an increasing population and peoples' need to be housed close to their work places.

One could be critical about the way urban sprawl was permitted to take place. With more thought and sensitivity, the original village identities could have been preserved for the benefit of the occupants. This is not an example of lost or deserted villages, it is more a case of villages losing their identity and individuality.

The larger towns in the county have all expanded and extended their boundaries to absorb adjoining communities. Even communities outside these boundaries but close to them are so contiguous that visitors would not know where the town boundaries are.

As one would expect, Derby has extended its boundaries from time to time, and in so doing has absorbed one time villages, some going back as far as Domesday. To some extent these villages have retained their identity as separate communities, usually when the parish church has survived as a living entity.

The identifiable one time villages absorbed by the now City of Derby are:

Osmaston-by-Derby	see Chapter 10
Normanton (by-Derby)	Church - SK347337
Littleover	Church - SK333342
Allestree	Church - SK348398
Chaddesden	Church - SK382369
Megaloughton	Possible lost village SK3934
Alvaston	Church - SK393334
Crewton	SK3733

Boulton	Hall? SK384330 now lost
Allenton	Church - SK371319
Little Chester	Derventio - see Chapter 4
Litchurch	SK3436

Chesterfield, now the county's second largest town, has sprawled and absorbed a few village sites, mostly already destroyed by the Earl of Leicester "for his pleasure", see Chapter 10. Given that these may have partially repopulated, they are still remembered by the suburbs and urban sprawl containing Hady, Newbold, Boythorpe and Hasland. To this could be added the conjoining areas of Whittington, Dunston, Tapton, Walton and Brimington although some of these have kept their village identity.

Glossop is an excellent example of how urbanisation during the industrialisation of the area encroached on adjoining villages but retained the individuality of each community. In this sense these did not become lost communities. At the time of Domesday Glossop and all the adjoining villages were "waste", but some were repopulated and still exist as part of an area we tend to refer to collectively as Glossop. The original Glossop exists as Old Glossop, a charming backwater at SK0494 to the west of which is the new Glossop formed in the last century around a group of mills which took advantage of the waters of the River Etherow. This community was much influenced by the industrialisation of nearby Manchester. Longdendale was "waste, fit only for hunting" in Domesday and this has not changed although the valley bottom is drowned by a string of reservoirs: Woodhead, Torside, Rhodeswood and Valehouse.

Of the villages which were waste in Domesday, most seem to have been repopulated and exist today as hamlets;

Thornsett - lost but somewhere between Hayfield and Glossop

Ludworth - no longer in Derbyshire

Charlesworth - now a village but the church built on the site of a chapel at SK011927 suggests an earlier settlement.

Chisworth - SJ997923 now a mill settlement.

Ludworth - SJ9990 and SJ9991 now known as Ludworth Intakes and Moor respectively, now no longer part of Derbyshire but were at the time of Domesday.

Hadfield - a nineteenth century mill community northwest of Glossop at SK0296

Padfield - ditto north of Glossop at SK0396

Dinting   - hamlet outside Glossop at SK0294

Whitfield - a nineteenth century mill community south of Glossop at SK0393.

All were waste at the time of Domesday.

BIBLIOGRAPHY

The following books were consulted and are available through local public libraries all now being out of print, apart from Mee and Morgan:

Beresford, M W
The Lost Villages of England   Lutterworth Press, 1954-63

Beresford, M W and Hurst, J G
Deserted Medieval Villages   Lutterworth Press, 1968

Muir, Richard
The Lost Villages of Britain   Michael Joseph, 1986

Craven,M and Stanley, M
The Derbyshire Country House   Derbys Museum Service, 1982
ditto Volume II   ditto   1984

Morgan, P ed.
Domesday Book, Derbyshire   Phillimore, 1978

Frith, J B
Highways and Byways of Derbyshire   Macmillan, 1920

Gill, G
The Story of the Lost Villages   Private, 1947

Mee, A
The King's England, Derbyshire   Hodder & Stoughton, 1974

Rodgers, F
Curiosities of the Peak District   Moorland Publishing, 1979
                                                Derbyshire Countryside,1992

Sanders, N
A Walkers Guide to the Upper Derwent   PPJPB,1984

Naylor, P J
Celtic Derbyshire   Halls, 1983

Naylor P J
Derbyshire Graves   Watnay, 1992

Naylor, P J
Ancient Wells and Springs of Derbyshire   Scarthin, 1983

Ordnance Survey Maps - 1:50,000 Landranger Series -

Sheet 109 - Manchester
Sheet 119 - Buxton, Matlock and Dovedale
Sheet 120 - Mansfield and Worksop
Sheet 121 - Derby and Leicester
Sheet 128 - Derby and Burton upon Trent

The Dark Peak - Outdoor Leisure Map   1:25,000 series
The White Peak   - ditto

INDEX

The deserted villages referred to in this book are indexed here with grid references and chapter numbers. The grid references are also mentioned in the text and are six figure wherever possible using the church wherever existing, failing which the village centre or the surviving manor or farm is given as near as possible. Where the location is large or indefinable a four figure reference is given within which square the location may be found. The villages marked 'unknown' refers to villages mentioned in Domesday, the sites of which have yet to be established.

VILLAGE	GRID REF:	CHAPTER:
Abney Grange	SK191787	8
Aldwark Grange	SK229572	8
Alkmonton	SK196386	6
Allenton	SK371319	12
Allestree	SK348398	12
Alvaston	SK393334	12
Anavio	See Brough	
Ardotalia	SK009951	4
Arleston	SK335297	9
Ash (or Ashe)	SK261326	6
Ashopton	SK194864	11
Ault Hucknall	SK466652	10
Ballidon	SK2054	9
Barbrook	SK272782	3
Barton Blount	SK209346	1 & 10
Bearwoodcote	SK283334	9
Bentley, Hungry	see Hungry Bentley	
Biggin	SK147590	8
Birchill	SK226707	9
Bolun	unknown	5
Boythorpe	SK3870	10
Boulton	SK384330	12
Bradbourne Grange	SK210525	8
Bradley	SK3547	5
Bretby	SK300225	10
Brough (Navio)	SK182828	4
Bubnell	SK248726	9
Bupton	SK224374	6
Burley	SK276643	9
Burton	SK220677	10
Callow	SK269518	9
Calke	SK369223	10
Calton	SK685245	10
Catton	SK207155	10

VILLAGE	GRID REF:	CHAPTER:
Cellesdene	see Chelton	
Chaddesden	SK382369	12
Charlsworth	SK011927	12
Chatsworth	SK257702	10
Chelton	unknown	5
Chisworth	SJ997923	12
Chunal	SK034917	6
Cold Eaton	see Eaton, Cold	
Conksbury	SK208657	1 & 8
Cotes in Darley	unkown	9
Cottons	SK3532	9
Coweley	SK253632	9
Crewton	SK3733	12
Derventio (Little Chester)	SK353376	4 & 12
Derwent	SK185885	11
Dinting	SK0294	12
Drakelow	SK2420	9
Dunsley	SK269569	2
Dunston	SK365745	10
Eastwood	SK258629	9
Eaton Dovedale	SK109373	9
Eaton, Cold	SK148567	6
Eddlestow	SK328631	9
Egstow	SK392649	10
Elvaston	SK411325	10
Farley	SK294623	9
Foremark	SK330265	10
Gardoms Edge	SK2773	3
Gratton	SK208618	8
Greyhurst	unknown	5 & 10
Griffe Grange	SK253564	8
Haddon, Nether	SK235665	10
Hadfield	SK0292	12
Hanson Grange	SK152545	8
Hardstoft	SK457633	10
Hardwick Grange	SK462637	8 & 10
Harewood Grange	SK312680	8
Harthill	SK230646	5 & 8
Hazelbadge	SK171800	10
Heathcote Grange	SK1460	8
Holme	SK354724	10
Hoon	SK224299	9
	or SK230316	9
Hopwell	SK440363	10
Houghpark	SK241464	10
Hulland, Upper	SK249475	10

VILLAGE	GRID REF:	CHAPTER:
Hungry Bentley	SK180388	6
Ireton Parva	SK314415	10
Ingleby	SK350270	9
Ivonbrook Grange	SK245585	8
Kedleston	SK312405	10
Kidsley	SK416459	
Langley	unknown	5
Lea	SK195517	6
Leash Fen	SK2973	2
Litchurch	SK3436	
Little Chester	see Derventio	
Littleover	SK333342	12
Longford	SK215383	10
Longdendale	SK0297 to SK0999	5
Ludwell	SK124623	3
Ludworth	SJ9990/9991	12
Lutudaron (et var)	SK2552	4
Makeney	SK353447	9
Mam Tor	SK128937	3
Mapleton	SK165480	10
Marsh	SK395305	5
Meadow Place Grange	SK201658	8
Megaloughton	SK3934	12
Melandra	see Ardotalia	
Mercaston	SK278424	8
Meynell Langley	SK301398	10
Middleton Grange	SK1963	8
Mouldridge Grange	SK202594	8
Muchedeswell	unknown	5
Navio	see Brough	
Nether Haddon	see Haddon, Nether	
Normanton	SK347337	12
Offcote	SK204480	8
Okeover	SK158481	10
One Ash Grange	SK169653	8
Osmaston-by-Derby	SK369338	10 & 12
Overton	SK345623	9
Owlcotes	SK422680	9
Padfield	SK0393	12
Padinc	unknown	5
Pickering	SK238658	10
Pilsbury Castle	SK113638	1
Potlock	SK313287	9
Potter Somersall	see Somersall, Potter	
Priestcliffe	SK140720	9
Ravensholm	unknown	5
Roystone Grange	SK204480	1 & 8

VILLAGE	GRID REF:	CHAPTER:
Sapperton	SK186345	6
Scarcliffe Grange	SK500701	8
Scarthin	SK295569	10
Sedsall	SK111376	9
Shuckstonfield	SK3656	
Sinfin	SK342312	9
Smithycote	SK4349	5
Snodeswick	unknown	5
Soham	unknown	5
Somersall	SK354699	10
Somersall, Potter	SK143353	9
Stanton Moor	SK2463	3
Stainsby	SK449656	10
Stoke	SK239769	9
Sturston	SK202467	7
Thornsett	unknown	5 & 12
Thulston	SK414317	10
Tunstall	unknown	5 & 10
Uftonfields	SK397563	9
Uluritune	unknown	5
Underwood	SK197484	1 & 6
Upton	unknown	5
Walton	SK359691	5 & 10
Waterfield	SK1779	5
Welledene	unknown	5
Werredune	unknown	5
Wessington Grange	SK3757	8
Whitfield	SK0393	12
Wigwell Grange	SK305544	8
Willersley	SK298572	10

Also by the author:

Discover Lost Mines	1981
Discover Dowsing and Divining	1980/87/91/93/97
Ancient Wells and Springs of Derbyshire	1983
Celtic Derbyshire	1983
Manors and Families of Derbyshire (Two Volumes)	1984
Grandfather Thomas Jackson's Recipes	1985
Derbyshire Graves	1992
The Derbyshire Connections of the Stokely Family of Iowa, USA	1987
Map of Ashbourne, 1900	1994
Cromford - A History	1997
Bulletin of the Peak District Mines Historical Society (several contributions)	1972 to 1983

Commissioning Specialists' Association - Technical Memoranda

TM3: Design of Standard Test Sheets	1993
TM7: Steam and the Commissioning Engineer	1994
TM9: Water Treatment and the Commissioning Engineer	1993

<u>Derbyshire Heritage Series -</u>

ANGLO-SAXON & VIKING DERBYSHIRE *by Richard Bunting.*
ARTISTS WITH DERBYSHIRE CONNECTIONS *by Harold Fearnehough*
BUXTON WATERS - A history of Buxton *by M.Langham & C. Wells*
THE CAPTIVE QUEEN IN DERBYSHIRE - Mary Queen of Scots - *by E.Eisenberg*
CASTLE & MANORS IN AND AROUND DERBYSHIRE *by Mike Smith*
CELTIC DERBYSHIRE *by Peter J. Naylor*
CHURCHES OF DERBYSHIRE *by John J. Anderson .*
DERBY CHINA THROUGH THREE CENTURIES *by Myra Challand*
DERBY CITY STREET TO STREET GUIDE
DERBYSHIRE CHARACTERS FOR YOUNG PEOPLE *by E. Eisenberg*
DERBYSHIRE CHURCHYARDS *by Joyce Critchlow .*
DERBYSHIRE'S MONASTIC HERITAGE *by Michael Smith*
DERBYSHIRE NOTEBOOK - *illustrated by E. Kazimierczuk*
DERBYSHIRE SUPERLATIVES *by Julie Bunting*
THE DERBYSHIRE YEAR - Customs through the years - *by E. Eisenberg*
EYAM, THE PLAGUE AND AN 1858 RAMBLE *by Clarence Daniel*
FLORENCE NIGHTINGALE *by Norma Keen*
FROM THE CRADLE TO THE GRAVE *by E. Eisenberg*
GAZETTER OF THE WHITE PEAK *by Les Robson*
GRANDFATHER THOMAS JACKSON'S RECIPES *by Thomas Jackson*
MANORS & FAMILIES OF DERBYSHIRE *Vol 1 (A - L)*
MANORS & FAMILIES OF DERBYSHIRE *Vol 2 (M - Z)*
MAY THE LORD HAVE MERCY ON YOUR SOUL *by Phillip Taylor*
NOTABLE DERBYSHIRE FAMILIES - family history - *by Roy Christian*
THE OWNERS OF MELBOURNE HALL *by Howard Usher*
THE PEAKLAND ABeCeDARY *by Jule Bunting*
PEAKLAND CHRONOLOGY *by Julie Bunting*
PREHISTORIC DERBYSHIRE *by Gerda & John Pickin*
RIVERS OF DERBYSHIRE *by Harold Fearnehough*
ROMAN DERBYSHIRE *by John Anderson*
STUART DERBYSHIRE *by Joy Childs*
SWARKESTONE BRIDGE & THE STANTON CAUSEWAY *by G.R. Heath*
THIS COSTLY COUNTESS - Bess of Hardwick - *by E. Eisenberg*
TUDOR DERBYSHIRE *by Joy Childs*
WALK THROUGH DERBY - *facsimile first published in 1827*

THE WATER CURE *by Alan Bower*
WOMEN OF DERBYSHIRE *by Susan Watson*
WORK & PLAY - Derbyshire, a photographic record - *by Alan Bower*
WRITERS WITH DERBYSHIRE CONNECTIONS *by Jane Darrall*
SPAGHETTI & BARBED WIRE - True World War 11 escapes story -
by Jack E. Fox
DERBYSHIRE GRAVES - 100 true and unusual graves - *by Peter Naylor*
ON THIS DAY....IN DERBYSHIRE - events that happened throughout the
year - *by John E. Heath*
THE EARLS AND DUKES OF DEVONSHIRE *by Julie Bunting*
TIMMY GLASS WAISTCOAT - Early 20th century life in Clay Cross
recalled - *by Jack E. Fox*
COAL, CHOCOLATE & CHIPS - 1940's and 50's life in Ripley -
by Aileen Watson.
JOHN SMEDLEY of Matlock *by John Large.*
STORIES OF THE DERBYSHIRE DALES *by John Large*
JOSEPH PAXTON *by John Large*
DERBYSHIRE STAINED GLASS WINDOWS - *by Dr. Joyce Critchlow*
LOST VILLAGES OF DERBYSHIRE - *by Peter Naylor*
CROMFORD - A HISTORY - *by Peter Naylor*
THE WEAVERS KNOT - life in the mills of North Derbyshire fictionalised
by Rosie Fellows
ELERGY OF AN EDWARDIAN CHILDHOOD IN DERBYSHIRE - Glossop
area - *by Ian Harlow*
SPIT, POLISH AND BULL - life in Clay Cross continued - *by Jack E. Fox*
A PEAKLAND WILDLIFE YEAR *by Richard Bunting*
COUNTRY POETRY *by Leslie Williamson*
NORMAN & MEDIEVAL DERBYSHIRE *by Richard Bunting*
THE CIVIL WAR IN THE TRENT VALLEY *by Andrew Polkey*

OTHER JOHN MERRILL BOOKS FROM Happy Walking International Ltd.,

CIRCULAR WALK GUIDES -
SHORT CIRCULAR WALKS IN THE PEAK DISTRICT - Vol 1,2 and 3
CIRCULAR WALKS IN WESTERN PEAKLAND
SHORT CIRCULAR WALKS IN THE STAFFORDSHIRE MOORLANDS
SHORT CIRCULAR WALKS - TOWNS & VILLAGES OF THE PEAK DISTRICT
SHORT CIRCULAR WALKS AROUND MATLOCK
SHORT CIRCULAR WALKS IN "PEAK PRACTICE COUNTRY."
SHORT CIRCULAR WALKS IN THE DUKERIES
SHORT CIRCULAR WALKS IN SOUTH YORKSHIRE
SHORT CIRCULAR WALKS IN SOUTH DERBYSHIRE
SHORT CIRCULAR WALKS AROUND BUXTON
SHORT CIRCULAR WALKS AROUND WIRKSWORTH
SHORT CIRCULAR WALKS IN THE HOPE VALLEY
40 SHORT CIRCULAR WALKS IN THE PEAK DISTRICT
CIRCULAR WALKS ON KINDER & BLEAKLOW
SHORT CIRCULAR WALKS IN SOUTH NOTTINGHAMSHIRE
SHIRT CIRCULAR WALKS IN CHESHIRE
SHORT CIRCULAR WALKS IN WEST YORKSHIRE
WHITE PEAK DISTRICT AIRCRAFT WRECKS
CIRCULAR WALKS IN THE DERBYSHIRE DALES
SHORT CIRCULAR WALKS FROM BAKEWELL
SHORT CIRCULAR WALKS IN LATHKILL DALE
CIRCULAR WALKS IN THE WHITE PEAK
SHORT CIRCULAR WALKS IN EAST DEVON
SHORT CIRCULAR WALKS AROUND HARROGATE
SHORT CIRCULAR WALKS IN CHARNWOOD FOREST
SHORT CIRCULAR WALKS AROUND CHESTERFIELD
SHORT CIRCULAR WALKS IN THE YORKS DALES - Vol 1 - Southern area.
SHORT CIRCULAR WALKS IN THE AMBER VALLEY (Derbyshire)
SHORT CIRCULAR WALKS IN THE LAKE DISTRICT
SHORT CIRCULAR WALKS IN THE NORTH YORKSHIRE MOORS
SHORT CIRCULAR WALKS IN EAST STAFFORDSHIRE
DRIVING TO WALK - 16 Short Circular walks south of London by Dr. Simon Archer Vol 1 and 2
LONG CIRCULAR WALKS IN THE PEAK DISTRICT - Vol.1,2 and 3.
WHITE PEAK AIRCRAFT WRECK WALKS
LONG CIRCULAR WALKS IN THE STAFFORDSHIRE MOORLANDS
LONG CIRCULAR WALKS IN CHESHIRE
WALKING THE TISSINGTON TRAIL
WALKING THE HIGH PEAK TRAIL
WALKING THE MONSAL TRAIL & OTHER DERBYSHIRE TRAILS
40 WALKS WITH THE SHERWOOD FORESTER by Doug Harvey
PEAK DISTRICT WALKING - TEN "TEN MILER'S"

CANAL WALKS -
VOL 1 - DERBYSHIRE & NOTTINGHAMSHIRE
VOL 2 - CHESHIRE & STAFFORDSHIRE
VOL 3 - STAFFORDSHIRE
VOL 4 - THE CHESHIRE RING
VOL 5 - LINCOLNSHIRE & NOTTINGHAMSHIRE
VOL 6 - SOUTH YORKSHIRE
VOL 7 - THE TRENT & MERSLY CANAL
VOL 8 - WALKING THE DERBY CANAL RING

JOHN MERRILL DAY CHALLENGE WALKS -
WHITE PEAK CHALLENGE WALK
DARK PEAK CHALLENGE WALK
PEAK DISTRICT END TO END WALKS

WHILE IN THE PEAK DISTRICT VISIT JOHN MERRILL'S HAPPY WALKING SHOP, LATHKILL DALE CRAFT CENTRE, OVER HADDON, NR. BAKEWELL

For a full list of titles - more than 300 - write for a free catalog to-

Happy Walking International Ltd., Unit 1, Molyneux Business Park, Whitworth Road, Darley Dale, Matlock, Derbyshire.
DE4 2HJ